# Ten Dancers

# Ten

### Text by

# Holly Brubach

A Seaver Book
William Morrow and Company, Inc.
New York    1982

On stage,
backstage,
at home,
and on the road

# Dancers

# Photographs by
# Pierre Petitjean

DO NOT

SIT

ON

STAIRS

By the author of
BACKSTAGE

Library of Congress Cataloging in Publication Data

Petitjean, Pierre, 1947-
    Ten dancers.

    "A Seaver book."
    1. Ballet dancing.   I. Brubach, Holly.
II. Title.
GV1787.P483          792.8′2′0922        81-22552
ISBN 0-688-01216-7        AACR2

Printed in the United States of America
First Edition

1  2  3  4  5  6  7  8  9  10

Book designed by Lesley Achitoff

To the memory of my father
To my mother, to my wife, Copette,
and to my children, Stephane, Julien and
Anne Sophie

# Acknowledgments

For their kind assistance, my gratitude and thanks to the American Ballet Theatre; the New York City Ballet; the Paris International Dance Festival; the Carpentras Festival; Lady Sainsbury, Chairman of the Friends of One-Parent Families (England); to my good friend François Letaconnoux, who helped me throughout the long search that was the making of this book; and finally, a special thanks to Jeannette Seaver, who has always shown so much understanding of my work.

# Contents

There are ten dancers here. That might as easily have been nine or eleven, or only two, or even forty. The point, however, is not how many but who—and that decision was made by the photographer, Pierre Petitjean, or perhaps by his camera. His roster is not necessarily the "top ten." They are dancers who have captured his eye and held his interest throughout countless performances, in some cases over a period of several years. So varied are their styles of performing that it is doubtful any one dance-goer would be willing to label all ten of them "great."

But taken all together, these dancers have won awards and gold medals, made front-page headlines and magazine covers, performed in every major opera house in the world (and a good many high-school auditoriums), provided the greatest choreographers at work today with inspiration. Not only are they dancers, they are celebrities. Even so, it is not their fame that sets them apart from ballet's rank and file. Their distinction lies in their dancing. On a full stage, in a huge company, we would—easily, inevitably—single any one of them out. They compel our attention.

The original premise for this book was a visual one: Petitjean conceived of photographs that would show a single dancer at home, taking class, making up, and performing—arranged in such a way that we might witness the transformation from the more-or-less ordinary person who looks like anybody's next-door neighbor to the extraordinary, larger-than-life dancer we see onstage. That metamorphosis was the intended subject of this book—in pictures. And that subject is certainly here: the curtain has been pulled aside and we, the audience, are

# Introduction

allowed to watch the daily ritual, the elaborate preparation that culminates in performance.

But, as so often happens with images assembled to illustrate one idea, these photographs also suggest another. What emerges from any one of these ten series is the dancer's unmistakable identity: the glamorous creature Natalia Makarova becomes onstage is clearly the same woman we glimpse at a party; the Peter Martins we see at ease, wearing running shoes, at home, with his bicycle parked in his living room, and the Martins pictured dancing *Apollo* are, undoubtedly, one and the same. So, instead of confirming the popularly held notion that great dancers are godlike, these photographs in some ways bring dancers down to earth. Which might seem to some fans a loss or, at the very least, a betrayal—as sweat can be when it belies a dancer's effortless grace. But the hard facts of a dancer's life are not necessarily disheartening.

If anything, the truth makes a better story than the fiction.

Supposing dancers aren't superhuman after all. Then this transformation they undergo must lie within the range of possibilities we all share. There are no shortcuts to becoming a great dancer—perpetual hard work is the only route. If the story these pictures tell has a moral, it is that dancing is not the mystical business it's so often made out to be, that ballet, for all its romantic illusion, is in fact a carefully conceived plan that, like architecture, takes into account physical limits and the laws of gravity. The building material is the human body.

In its way, ballet may fulfill our longing to be other than what we are and, at the same time, make us realize how fine it is to be human. It is this contradiction which lies at the heart of a great performance—and at the heart of these photographs.

1

What distinguishes a dancer, what sets a Makarova or a Van Hamel or a Dowell apart from the corps de ballet? A survey of the ten dancers here turns up more differences than similarities. Some of them share a hobby (Makarova and Van Hamel both paint, for example), some have a common background (Van Hamel and Thesmar are both the daughters of diplomats). Four of these ten were raised by their mothers; their parents had either divorced or separated. But none of these statistics would seem to have much bearing on how a person dances.

Nor is there any one physical type that guarantees great dancing. The five women here range from petite to tall, slight to voluptuous; the men, of various heights, from brawny to lithe. There are pale blonds, dark brunettes. These dancers come from England, France, Russia, Denmark, Belgium, and the United States, by way of a good many other countries where they grew up or studied ballet or worked as dancers. Perhaps the only significant statistic for this group is that eight of the ten have migrated to New York and are now based there. From England's Royal Ballet, from the Kirov and the Bolshoi, from the Royal Danish Ballet, the National Ballet of Canada, they have come to work in the city that is now the acknowledged dance capital. The styles and schools in which they were trained are as diverse as their backgrounds (only two, McBride and Bujones, attended the same school, the School of American Ballet in New York, but even their similarity ends there—McBride was graduated into the New York City Ballet, and Bujones joined the American Ballet Theatre).

Perhaps the only sweeping statement to be made about these ten dancers is that they are all distinct individuals. For all the different identities they are capable of assuming onstage, there is no mistaking any one of them for somebody else.

Classical ballet, with its precise positions and rigorous discipline, can sometimes seem confining to a child beginning lessons. There is one way to execute a

## The Photographs

step correctly; every other way is wrong. If a student must cut a few corners and blur a few positions in order to get through a combination, getting through becomes inconsequential. If a girl can raise her leg six inches higher simply by shifting her weight into the supporting hip, that doesn't count. For the first few years of training, this insistence on clean technique at all costs is overwhelming. It takes years to acquire the muscular control, the coordination, and the strength necessary to maintain this precision in motion.

Though some dancers emerge in their teens with a seemingly complete technique, they must spend the rest of their careers maintaining and perfecting it, practicing a handful of steps that are difficult for them personally, adding more turns or beats, pushing their extension or their jump ever higher. Other dancers come into their technique more slowly, and only after several years on the stage do they manage to master certain troublesome steps.

Most dancers have a natural predisposition to fast or slow movement, lyrical phrasing or sharp attack which stays with them throughout their careers. Some dancers fill the gaps, acquiring what doesn't come naturally to them by hard work. Others stay closer to "home," dancing within the range their physiques and temperaments have staked out for them, learning whatever else is required well enough to tide them over from strength to strength. Each of the ten dancers in this book is technically proficient, but technique isn't everything. It's not even prerequisite to greatness. There may well be dancers in the corps capable of more *pirouettes* or a higher *développé*, but that alone doesn't make them command our attention.

"I'm not sure what it is that makes one dancer stand out from all the rest," Martine van Hamel says, "but you can definitely see it. It has something to do with their individual qualities—who they are, the way they move. We're all given the same vocabulary as dancers, but from there on it's up to the individual, to his or her own interpretation. Also, I think a stage presence makes a

3

difference. I don't really know where it comes from, I think maybe you're born with it. You can develop it to a certain extent, but it must be something you have inside you, something you must express. Most of the dancers who are interesting to watch are really involved in performing, they're totally absorbed in dancing when they're out there onstage, and that consistently carries across the footlights."

At some point along the way, the dancers here reconciled their own personalities to the technique of classical ballet, which is abstract, general, impersonal. They learned to relax and express themselves within its parameters. They came to think in terms of ballet movements, so that even the most difficult steps would seem second-nature, never artificial or forced. And then, having appropriated this classical vocabulary, they went on about their dancing, saying whatever it is they have to say in ballet's terms. Ghislaine Thesmar explains, "It is while dancing that I have felt the most perfect harmony between myself and everything that I love."

To Alexander Godunov's way of thinking, it's "talent and personality" that distinguish a dancer. Also, "hard work—if and when God gives you the talent, you must work at it to keep it. Brains are also very important, in terms of how you use your gift. You must become a work of art, but with brains and a soul. You must be technically wonderful, but you must have more. You must be able to touch your audience.

"Onstage, a dancer is naked, and everything that is going on in his life is transformed in his dancing. You must use the energies of your life experience in your performance. But only with brains can you develop the ability to transform that energy into art."

The steps must be made clear, but with such authority that they seem to belong solely to the dancer. Every classical role bears the imprints of the great dancers who, within our memory, made it their own. It is impossible for many ballet fans to watch *The Sleeping Beauty* without seeing reminders of Margot Fonteyn in the role of Aurora. No one who witnessed Rudolf Nureyev in *Le Corsaire,* even on film, can evaluate another dancer in the role without comparing his interpretation to Nureyev's. In the Balanchine repertory, Edward Villella's looks and style have become the yardstick by which veterans measure other dancers' performances. A good choreographer devises steps in his dancers' images. So, we can look at Sir Frederick Ashton's *Birthday Offering* and see in the dancing portraits of its original cast. Watching George Balanchine's *Divertimento No. 15* today, we see not only the dancers in the present cast, who have laid their own claim to their variations, but previous casts as well: one role is, over the years, refracted to yield images of several dancers, all at once.

"What makes a distinguished artist," Fernando Bujones speculates, "is perhaps the uniqueness one can bring to the dance world." His own uniqueness, he believes, lies in "a certain polish and a clean outlook—others bring a Romantic air or spectacular technique or

something else special. And all this, together, makes the dance world a larger place."

This dance world is, simply, the world in dance. Contrary to the ethereal stereotype, some ballerinas are big and forceful; some are witty; some are athletic; some sexy; some lazy. There are as many kinds of people who dance as there are kinds of people.

Many—but not all—distinguished dancers are singled out early, in the first few years of their careers or in classes, before they begin performing. Often, the basis for this first attention is purely physical—a beautiful instep, naturally high extension, easy spring in a jump. This is the raw material, worth little in and of itself, but in the hands of the right dancer (and the right teacher), it may become remarkable. So children will attract notice not because they've accomplished anything, but because they have the potential to accomplish a great deal. The notice is in itself a form of encouragement.

There is a hierarchy implicit in most dance classes, evident in the places assigned at the barre or in the center. To be at the head of the class is an honor, even in dancing. Some students rise to such high expectations: this is a performing art, after all, and it stands to reason that the dancer who thinks that all eyes are on him will work harder than the one who thinks no one is watching. So a pattern, a cycle in which work is rewarded by special attention and the encouragement to work more is established while a dancer is still in his formative years. If this cycle continues unbroken, the momentum may propel him right out of the studio and onto the stage, into principal roles. That is the route by which several of these ten dancers arrived.

But not all dancers fulfill what they promise; some bristle at close attention, or they get anxious, scared. The teacher's steady gaze, which may make one dancer feel secure, may make another feel pressured, as if he must produce—a higher jump, more beats—or prove himself. So some dancers fall behind, for reasons that have nothing to do with their physical capabilities. Some fall by the wayside: though they dance full-time, professionally, they withdraw from the running for lead roles and high ranks, content to live out their careers in the corps.

And then there are those dancers who weren't the obvious candidates from the start, who came to class faithfully and worked diligently until, little by little, they assembled a technique and an identity in their dancing, and emerged. These dancers burst upon an audience: we watch them for years and then, suddenly, we actually see them for the first time.

Of course, once a dancer is on the stage, in the public eye, the cycle that began in a teacher's expectations picks up speed. The press gives it an extra push. Then it's the audience whose attention is focused on that dancer. There is speculation at intermission, an occasional encouraging mention in reviews.

Patricia McBride thinks distinction is in the eye of the beholder. "It's a matter of personal taste," she says, "like movie stars or opera singers or pianists. I've heard opera fans arguing Callas versus Tebaldi—who is the greatest. But I've always felt that there are so many different kinds of beauty in the world. Each person in the audience, each critic, each choreographer has his own particular taste in dance." For example, the ranks of the New York City Ballet reflect George Balanchine's personal taste. "It's his company—he chooses who he wants to see dancing certain roles. The company is filled with so many beautiful dancers, and those that he maybe hasn't liked often go elsewhere and do very well. But, I must say, he does have a marvelous eye for talent."

There is, unavoidably, some talent that goes unrecognized; some dancers who simply find themselves in the wrong place at the wrong time. A successful career, McBride says, can largely depend on vehicles. "A dancer needs to be seen in the right ballets—that's very important. And having ballets made on you is, of course, an ideal situation. I think a good role is the most wonderful gift a dancer can receive. It's like a head start, to be dancing in a masterpiece, in a role so good that it almost runs by itself.

"I've never analyzed myself," she continues, "never decided, 'Well, this is the sort of dancer I am.' I don't really think about what it is people see in my dancing. I'm actually very selfish—I just adore to dance. Still."

Besides vehicles, McBride concedes, "a dancer needs publicity." The power and extent of the press are not to be underestimated in this era, when magazines are busy marketing "life-styles" and celebrity is a full-time job. The ten dancers here are also stars, though they vary in magnitude.

Patrick Dupond admits that "it's scary to be so successful at twenty-one. Fame is, of course, an increasing responsibility. There is a lot of interest in dance and in dancers' lives. As a *danseur étoile,* I am no longer anonymous, but even today, the names of singers and musicians mean more to the audience than those of dancers who have reached the same level. Dancers need more publicity."

Some actively cultivate their own fame; others neglect it, and it grows regardless. Most of these ten employ a manager, who books their private guest appearances, and a publicist or a personal secretary, to field interviews and other matters that are not bookings. (This personal support staff is in addition to the publicists and managers attached to the ballet companies these dancers belong to.) Like actors and actresses, like opera singers, prominent dancers today are free-lance artists, hopping jets all over the world for one- or two-night stands, hiring themselves out to various companies who provide the context—the opera house, the grand-scale productions, the corps de ballet—in which they can perform principal roles. Big-name dancers help sell tickets; they lend their status, however temporarily, to the local company. Of course, there are more dance companies in the world today than there ever have been in any era before, and the demand for guest artists is practically unlimited. Why, then, would any dancer choose to subjugate himself to the management of a single company on a regular basis when he could virtually write his own ticket as a guest star?

The dancers in this book all agree on one issue: that no dancer can build a great career without a company he or she can call home. Some regard their companies as home bases, where they touch down and dance a few familiar roles between engagements abroad. Others are self-confessed homebodies, who venture away from their regular companies only on rare occasions.

Martine van Hamel says, "I think that if you're constantly guesting, it's very hard to keep your perspective, to keep your artistic growth and your ambitions in line. It's also much less secure—you never really know what or where your next job is. And you have none of the comforts and pleasures of being with a company."

Dupond regards guest appearances as a means of cramming more dancing into the short span of a career. At thirty-five or so, having performed all over the world, a dancer might then feel more willing to retire, satisfied that his career had been a full one. "One always has to make room for new dancers, and why not? Even the public gets bored seeing the same dancers every night." As a member of the Paris Opera Ballet, a government institution, Dupond is technically a civil servant. So, there is a certain "security in remaining with the company, but I am a rebel—I enjoy taking risks and experimenting. Ideally, one should be able to dance for this *maison mère* four or five months a year and then free-lance."

Many dancers strike a healthy balance between their work at home and abroad. Fernando Bujones believes that a company provides "the assurance of artistic maturity and the constant stream of new works" that a dancer might have a hard time finding on his own. "But I think it's also very important to 'guest,' because it provides a new atmosphere. By having gone out and danced the same ballet, but in different styles, with different companies, my own dancing has been enriched. In one production, the acting will be done one way, and in another, it will be slightly different—one always has to adapt oneself to a new company, and that is, in itself, an artistic achievement. Plus, there are certain ballets I don't have the chance to perform with my own company—the full-length *Romeo and Juliet,* for instance, has brought out a great deal in me as an actor."

Ghislaine Thesmar says, "I think a dancer needs very much a home in a real ballet company, with a real ballet master. I married the Paris Opera," she adds, "but my heart stayed with George Balanchine at the New York City Ballet."

The New York City Ballet is, in Patricia McBride's words, "my stability. I'm not the kind of person who could roam continually, from one company to the next. I love the City Ballet, and I love working with Balanchine and Jerry Robbins. But I need to go on the outside and do other things, too. I think it's good for a dancer to be on her own once in a while. And I'm never bored. Also, I have a certain repertory in City Ballet—I could probably be typed more easily than some of the other dancers. But when I go outside the company and do other ballets, I'm seen in a different light."

Alexander Godunov, a dancer who might have coasted as a guest artist on the publicity surrounding his defection, has chosen instead to do most of his performing within the context of the American Ballet Theatre. "Personally, I need a company," he explains. "You can be a guest for a long time—and you can be very strong about keeping your body in shape and practicing—but, eventually, you must spend time with a company and work with them, as part of an ensemble. Ballet is theater, and a dancer must have fellow performers—a corps—with whom he works on a regular basis. The company is also the place where a dancer perfects his art—where he can hone his technique and clean up his act. So, in that way, it even helps when the time comes to make guest appearances. A dancer can get along without a company today, but it means losing a lot."

Brief forays into other, slightly foreign styles of dancing raise all sorts of hypothetical questions. For one, what sort of a dancer would you be if you were with a different company? McBride answers, "I've often wondered about that. Even though I started taking ballet classes when I was very young, I went to the School of American Ballet when I was fourteen, and at sixteen, I became a professional and joined the New York City Ballet. So, from then on, Balanchine was my teacher. And, of course, being one of his dancers, I did a *glissade* the way he wants it done, did the technique as he wants to see it. The energy, the attack on the steps I learned from him. So, he may have developed me and made me the dancer I am today, but, as far as style goes, I think that's more personal—I think it's whatever we're born with."

That rank we call stardom seems inevitable for most of the dancers who attain it. But no matter how "natural" the dancer, how manifold his gifts, there is no escaping the work—it is the one constant in a life that changes from one minute to the next. No headlines, no opening-night parties, no curtain calls, no promotions, no foreign tours can alter the dancer's perspective, which is short-range: there is always class tomorrow morning.

Few people sitting in the ballet audience realize just how relentless the demands on a dancer really are. Six days a week begin with class in the morning, followed by rehearsals in the afternoon, and, depending on the

company and its schedule, a performance in the evening. There is little or no dinner until after the performance. A member of the New York City Ballet may enter the New York State Theater at ten in the morning and not leave until eleven that night, never seeing the light of day. The Opéra is like a city in itself, right in the middle of Paris: to walk from an administrative office to a rehearsal studio may take ten minutes. For dancers, the whole world may be only as large as the theater.

So it stands to reason that much of any dancer's personal life takes place within the theater, too. His best friends are, more often than not, other dancers, who share in his work and keep to the same schedule. Most dancers agree that the distinction between their professional and their personal lives is a vague one, that dancing usurps the spare time other people spend going to movies or playing tennis or dining out with friends.

"Even when I have free time," Godunov says, "I spend it thinking about dancing. To begin with, there is a barre and exercise, rehearsals, preparing new roles, resting for the performance, and the performance itself. Then there are all the other details—checking costumes, thinking about upcoming appearances. Even when I don't have to be at the studio or at the theater, I have to do interviews and have meetings about guest appearances. A certain amount of time must be spent socializing with the people you work with. Everything relates to your art, and you are always thinking about dance. You must keep your body in shape and you must prepare yourself mentally and emotionally for the performance. There is no real rest from dancing."

Dupond rehearses six to eight hours per day, when the Paris Opera is in season, and practices alone or with his teacher another two or three hours more. Few careers begin so early as dancing, and dancing is not so much a job as it is a way of life. "One's youth is burned, consumed, monopolized by only that one thing," he says. By his own estimate, he has five hundred books he's never had a chance to read, three hundred records he's never gotten around to listening to. "But now that I have reached this point"—the highest rank of *danseur étoile*—"I can start living, and I thirst for it."

Bujones, too, having established himself as a dancer, has gone on to make a stand for his personal life. "Perhaps sixty or seventy percent of my time is my dancing today, and the rest is my own personal life.

That's been one of the good things about my marriage—I have dedicated more time to outside activities and to my family than I used to, and I have been able to balance them with my dancing."

Not all marriages manage to stake out territory beyond the theater. Patricia McBride, whose husband is Jean-Pierre Bonnefous, another N.Y.C.B. principal dancer, says her career and her personal life are "all one. I can't really close off my professional life—it seems a part of me, the fact that I'm a dancer and not something else. So I don't leave it at the theater, I bring it home with me. But that doesn't mean I dance around the house. I love being at home. To look at our apartment, you'd never know we were dancers—we have no ballet photos, no souvenirs of our dance careers. It's a place apart. Not that I need to escape, because I'm very happy with my life—I love dancing and being in the theater. But we live with things that we love, and when we come in the door and we're greeted by our dog and cats, it's another world."

For Martine van Hamel, the distinction between professional and personal time is primarily territorial. "Fortunately, I can't dance at home," she explains. "I think about dancing sometimes, but that's as much as I can do if I'm not in a studio—I really do leave it behind when I come home." That time at home she fills with other interests—painting, though lately she's reached the point where all the space on her walls is filled; also, cooking. She would love a garden, but that's out of the question for most New Yorkers, "so I pretend with my plants, instead. I used to have a lot more free time, but now that I'm dancing so much I have less."

Ghislaine Thesmar is married to Pierre Lacotte, a choreographer. "My dancing and my personal life are equally important," she says, "and each feeds into the other."

The sacrifices dancing demands seem greater in the earlier stages of a dancer's career, in the struggle to acquire roles and to make a name for himself, when other boys and girls his age are comparatively carefree. But even with a sizable reputation and an international career that's off and running, a dancer must continually put dancing first. Alcohol and cigarettes, high-calorie desserts might seem relatively harmless, as vices go, but to dancers they represent something larger. It is the small, day-to-day decisions like these that keep a dancer's discipline in good working order, that keep him dancing at the top of his form.

Fatigue sets in. Hotel rooms are a poor substitute for home. An entire career in dance is only half as long as a lifetime. Why, then, do these ten people—and others—persist in dancing?

McBride believes in destiny. "I feel that I was born to do this."

Dupond says, "I don't know if I'll be the next Nijinsky, but I do know that I would like to be able to set the audience's nerves tingling and to make them experience my dancing at the same visceral level as I do."

Ghislaine Thesmar thinks that "dance must be the all-consuming passion of one's life. One must give it everything one has, if only for the ecstasy of a few sublime moments. Those moments are worth any price. I dance to honor life and the gifts God gave me."

How can photographs, which are motionless, tell us anything about dancing? The camera all too readily reduces a great ballet to a series of striking tableaux, the way the *Reader's Digest* abridges a novel. Meanwhile, the steps that connect those moments isolated in photos are passed over, forgotten. A breathtaking leap is preserved at its height; the takeoff and the landing fade away. Photographs show us still images, but it's between these images that the dancing lies. With nothing but photos to go on, our impressions of any single ballet or of any one dancer's performance would almost surely be mistaken.

But, despite its limitations, photography does dance more of a service than an injustice. It affords us that one luxury which an actual performance never allows: leisure. We can take our time looking at a picture of Alexander Godunov posed in *attitude*. The camera suspends Ghislaine Thesmar's jump. In poring over still photos of great dancers in action, observed in class, rehearsal, or performance, we learn what ballet is supposed to look like. The pictures here of Natalia Makarova rehearsing Giselle, poised in arabesque, would be well worth studying as a lesson in the Romantic style of dancing.

By looking at photographs, we come to a better understanding of the mechanics of dancing—which muscles generate certain movements, where support comes from, what proper placement is and what difference it

makes (Van Hamel's placement, in the glimpse we get of her here in class, or in performance, dancing *La Bayadère* with Patrick Bissell, is exemplary). In the picture of Peter Martins at the barre during company class, our eyes go immediately to his foot, which is strong and well

stretched. Another photo of Martins jumping, in a rehearsal of *Theme and Variations,* gives us a sense of the breath that helps to lift a dancer into the air. The picture of Cynthia Gregory dancing *Tchaikovsky Pas de Deux* with Fernando Bujones, snapped in arabesque and a split second before bursting into the next step, conveys the urgency that dancing fast requires.

The most obvious part still photography has played in the history of ballet has been to preserve the image of a great dancer for generations to come. Until quite recently, in fact, photos were the only record of ballets that had fallen by the wayside; now, of course, film and videotape are fast becoming commonplace for preserving choreography and performances. But whatever we know of Vaslav Nijinsky, Tamara Karsavina, Anna Pavlova, Isadora Duncan—dancers who, a mere seventy or so years ago, took audiences all over the world by storm— we have had to piece together from photographs. And, as anyone who has studied old dance photos can attest, it's surprising how much of a moving picture a single freeze-frame can suggest.

Some of the photos in this book are posed; others are candid. But none is intended as the sort of document dance photographs were in the past. Because this book is just as concerned with what takes place in the studio, on a bus, in the dressing room, in a supermarket or a boutique, as on the stage, the pictures here don't qualify as "dance photographs." Pierre Petitjean has photographed dancers and only in part their dancing. This book is a collection of character studies of ten people—ten dancers. We see Alexander Godunov testing a can of hair spray in an American drugstore, a shy-seeming Anthony Dowell at a party, with a drink in his hand, fingering the bottom of the glass. After the curtain has come down on *Fantaisie Sérieuse,* there is Makarova, still in costume, putting on what looks like a high-fashion flapper act for Dowell. The concentration written all over Fernando Bujones' face during class, the expression Van Hamel and Godunov share as they rehearse the "White Swan" pas de deux—these close-ups tell us more about who these people are than about how they dance.

There are, of course, those moments when these ten people come into their own, when they become totally themselves—usually, dancing. Patrick Dupond flies in a leap, stretched out over the front leg, like a kid who, having just discovered some amazing new feat, wants to show off for a friend. Peter Martins, rehearsing *Agon* with Heather Watts, supports her so intently that it seems as if her balance is all his responsibility. Warming up at the barre before a performance, Patricia McBride smiles straight into the camera—as direct and warm as she is onstage, taking a curtain call after *Le Baiser de la Fée.* While Baryshnikov was a member of the New York City Ballet, he and Martins got to be great friends. Here, a picture of them clowning in *Other Dances* shows them at ease, elegant—Baryshnikov deadpan, Martins about to set a joke in motion. Both stand with their legs crossed, arms folded; Baryshnikov seems a more compact version of Martins. In their identical stance, in Martins' head turned toward Baryshnikov, we read their fondness for each other.

Glamorous as these ten dancers look on the stage, that glamour is put on, like a costume, for the performance. But the steps dancers do in class are the same as those they do onstage. Bujones, in class with the Scottish Ballet in London, soars in a *grand jeté en attitude*—the front leg reaching forward, the back leg bent behind—in the same step he does onstage as James, in *La Sylphide.* Daily class, in addition to being the thorough workout every dancer needs to stay in shape, is also a practice

session, when dancers can work at mastering whatever steps they still find difficult, when they can continue to refine their techniques. Rehearsal is for learning new roles or reviewing old ones, for figuring out ways to execute the steps the choreographer requires. During class and in rehearsal, hard work and fatigue often go unconcealed, as these photographs prove. We look in on Van Hamel and Dowell taking class: both appear absolutely exhausted.

Photographs help us commit certain performances to memory, by zeroing in on one moment or on a single image that can somehow stand for an entire ballet. The picture of Peter Martins as Apollo, surrounded by the three Muses, is one example. Another is the picture of Thesmar as the Sylph, in an *arabesque penchée,* leaning flirtatiously on James's shoulder. Natalia Makarova, as Giselle, skips through Act I with a carefree girlishness that will become a woman's wisdom and compassion in the second act, when Giselle returns as a ghost.

While poses are not dancing, there are certain positions that mark the climax of a step or a phrase, and a good dance photographer needs a sense of timing almost as sophisticated as a dancer's to be able to recognize the precise moment when a movement is at its fullest. To miss that moment—at the height of a jump or the peak of a balance, when every line is fully stretched—is sometimes to take a picture of the dancing between positions. The photo here of Makarova in the first act of *Giselle* catches her coming down from the top of her skip, but before landing—the effect is, in this case, ingenuous, like Giselle herself.

Great dancers, like good dance photographers, know instinctively how to show us certain positions, leaving us with one image to savor until they've arrived at the next. They edit what we see.

Photographs may confirm the impression we already have of a certain dancer's performance or, when the pictures are of a dancer we've never seen, they may spark our curiosity. They are the only souvenirs of dancing we have. Even so, no seashell can take the place of being at the beach. Good dance photographs always refer to the live performance, sending us to the theater. And, having looked at these photographs, we go ready and able to take in more of the dancing than we ever saw before.

Anthony Dowell, a native of England's Royal Ballet, now spends the greater part of his dancing time with American Ballet Theatre, returning home occasionally during the Royal's London season or appearing with it on tour in the United States. To American audiences, he is the epitome of an English gentleman; he dances with a British accent. Debonair, eloquent, he shapes every step with meticulous attention to detail, rounding out the edges so that the end of one movement blends into the beginning of the next. He seems equally at ease in allegro and adagio. The boyish reticence that first characterized his dancing has in time given way to a new, more dramatic self-assurance, the innocence to introspection.

Dowell's mother had studied dancing, but never made a career of it. In hopes that her children might, she enrolled both Anthony (born in 1944) and his older sister in a local private school, in London, that offered dance as part of the curriculum. When, on his teacher's recommendation, he applied to the Royal Ballet School, Anthony was put through a simple barre and accepted immediately. He moved along—through the Royal's junior school, into the senior division, where students in their last year appear as supers in the company's performances at the Royal Opera House, Covent Garden. Dowell's debut came in *Swan Lake,* hunting with Prince Siegfried.

After graduation, he joined the Sadler's Wells Opera Ballet. Then, one year later, at eighteen, he received an invitation to the Royal. His first solo roles there—in Erik Bruhn's staging of the *Napoli* Divertissements, as the Country Boy in Andrée Howard's *La Fête Étrange*—soon led to larger parts: in Kenneth MacMillan's full-length *Romeo and Juliet,* Dowell created the role of Benvolio; in Sir Frederick Ashton's *The Dream,* he created Oberon. Titania was Antoinette Sibley, and in her Dowell seemed to find his perfect counterpart. He danced Romeo to her Juliet. Their proportions, their lines were ideally matched, their styles synonymous. Together, they brought new images and fresh interpretations to a repertory that had belonged, indisputably, to Rudolf Nureyev and Margot Fonteyn.

But when Sibley was forced by injuries to spend

# Anthony Dowell

more time on the sidelines than on the stage, Dowell went on to prove himself with other partners and alone. He moved into new roles in already familiar ballets: in MacMillan's *Manon,* in which he created Des Grieux, he set himself a further challenge in Lescaut. In *Romeo and Juliet,* he took on Mercutio. When, in 1976, Ashton choreographed Turgenev's *A Month in the Country,* it was with Dowell in the role of the earnest young tutor who comes and, in spite of himself, steals the hearts of the young boy he's meant to teach, the boy's mother, and the girl in her charge.

Periodically, A.B.T. would extend invitations to Dowell to appear as a guest artist and, with only one, one-time-only gala exception, he declined them all. Eventually, though, he began to contemplate a move to America in more serious, more permanent terms—an extended stay. When, in 1978, Dowell finally left the Royal Ballet, striking out on his own, he left home.

Like many dancers, Dowell has gone through periods of doubt about his own dancing—why do it? And, as for many dancers, those doubts were in his case accompanied by injuries, forcing him to take time off. He took advantage of the chance to pursue a second interest—costume design—and dressed John Curry's first ice show. (Dowell has also designed the costumes for Jerome Robbins' *In the Night,* at the New York City Ballet.) When the time came to ease his way back into dancing, Dowell did it under the close supervision of Winifred Edwards, one of his first teachers. Of his mentors, he credits much of his success to Michael Somes, for his coaching, and Derek Rencher, for his thoughtful conception of roles.

At A.B.T., Dowell has danced the full-length nineteenth-century classics—*Swan Lake, Giselle, Don Quixote, La Bayadère, The Nutcracker,* and more modern works by Robbins, Antony Tudor, Glen Tetley. He's continued his partnership with Makarova (begun at the Royal) and struck up a new one with Gelsey Kirkland, handling her sweet fragility with kid gloves. In 1980, Kirkland was invited to dance Juliet as a guest artist with the Royal Ballet, and Dowell returned as Romeo. Together, they brought the Royal Opera House down.

Dancing with Antoinette Sibley in Frederick Ashton's *Soupirs Pas de Deux*, London Palladium. 1980.

Dancing with Jennifer Penney in Kenneth MacMillan's *Waterfalls,* a pas de deux to music by Paul McCartney. London, 1980.

With Makarova in *Manon*. Washington, 1980.

Hugging Cynthia Harvey after a performance of *Don Quixote*.

With John Curry. Ebullient after the success of the premiere of Peter Gennaro's *Top Hat*. New York, 1979.

◄The world premiere of Lorca Massine's *Fantaisie Sérieuse*.

Makeup before Don Quixote. Washington, 1980.

◄Wig and makeup on, running through his final warm-up exercise before
appearing in *Manon.* Washington, 1979: in honor of the American Ballet
Theatre's fortieth anniversary.

Washington, 1980.

In his dressing room: with the typically British teapot. Washington, 1980.

Washington, 1980.

Washington, 1980.

With Makarova, exhausted after a rehearsal of *Fantaisie Sérieuse* at the old studios of the American Ballet Theatre on West Sixty-first Street. New York, 1980.

▲ Relaxing in his suite at the Watergate Hotel on his day off. Washington,
◄ 1980.

At a party given by Genia Doll, patroness of the Dance. New York. ▶

With Princess Margaret at a party at London's Park Lane Hotel following
a benefit gala at the London Palladium. 1980.

Natalia Makarova was born in Leningrad, in 1940, raised on Tchaikovsky Street by her mother and stepfather, a professional musician, and trained at the Vaganova School, which continually supplies the Kirov Ballet with some of the finest dancers in the world. (The Vaganova School occupies the same premises as the Imperial Ballet School did, before the revolution; the Kirov's theater is the old Maryinsky, where, in *Swan Lake, The Sleeping Beauty, La Bayadère, Raymonda, The Nutcracker,* Marius Petipa and Lev Ivanov laid the foundations for classical dancing as we know it.) But Makarova's career, which was, to say the least, auspicious in the Soviet Union, really began for Western audiences in 1961, when she first danced in London and New York, on tour. Then, nine years later, a new chapter began, when Makarova requested and was granted political asylum in London, on September 4, 1970. She went to rehearsal, to lunch, went shopping, then disappeared from view for a few days, until all the arrangements had been made final. The Kirov dancers, when told of her defection, reportedly wept.

Makarova repeatedly emphasized that her decision to defect had been dictated by the need for greater artistic freedom, though, as Soviet policy goes, she had been granted more liberties than most dancers—making occasional guest appearances in Europe, taking part in the making of new ballets at home. But the Soviet system of typecasting, or *emploi,* by which some dancers are labeled "classical," others "Romantic," others *"demi-caractère,"* according to physique and particular abilities, is in itself a restriction. Roles are assigned categorically. For Makarova, artistic freedom meant not only the opportunity to dance in works by Alvin Ailey or Antony Tudor, but in *The Sleeping Beauty,* as Aurora, or in *Don Quixote,* as Kitri—both roles she almost certainly would have been denied at the Kirov.

Soon after her defection, Makarova announced her decision to join American Ballet Theatre, although she has devoted nearly as much of her time to England's Royal Ballet—in their *Swan Lake,* in MacMillan's *Romeo and Juliet,* in Ashton's *A Month in the Country,* in (what many consider her greatest role) MacMillan's *Manon.* At

# $\mathcal{N}$atalia $\mathcal{M}$akarova

the Royal, Makarova first staged the fourth act of *La Bayadère,* "The Kingdom of the Shades," according to the choreography she had danced at the Kirov. In July, 1974, she mounted this same one-act version at A.B.T.; in 1980, she filled in the remaining acts for a complete, full-length production. The same year, she also organized her own small company, comprised of a handful of guest artists and a corps de ballet, for a four-week Broadway season. Makarova's partners at the Kirov included the late Yuri Soloviev and Mikhail Baryshnikov. When Baryshnikov followed Makarova to the West four years later, she sponsored him in his debut with Ballet Theatre, dancing Giselle to his Albrecht. Besides him, she has been paired in the West with Godunov, Anthony Dowell, Fernando Bujones, Rudolf Nureyev, Ivan Nagy (her favorite, formerly a principal dancer with A.B.T., now retired).

As a child, Makarova's fantasies were about growing up to be an actress, not a dancer, and she acted out tragedies in front of a full-length mirror. Not surprisingly, she is now acknowledged the great dramatic ballerina of our era, moving audiences to the point of heartbreak as a

frail, sensitive Giselle, an impetuous Juliet, a mesmerizing Odette, who, with her long, liquid arms and fluttering feet, is more swan than woman. Makarova was taught at the Kirov that a character's entire personality must be distilled in the way she walks, and to this day she begins building her notion of Giselle, of Juliet, of any role, by walking.

Under five feet three inches tall, Makarova, by virtue of her proportions—long neck, long arms, long legs—gives the impression of being tiny rather than short. She is blond, deceptively frail-looking but strong, with a pliant instep. Spontaneity is integral to her performing: some reactions, some events must be left to happen onstage. Consequently, her rendering of a role is never fixed. She is not one to duplicate her own great performance.

The normal course of study at the Vaganova School is nine years long, but Makarova, at age twelve, began later than usual in an experimental class of twenty-five girls put through the regular paces in a mere six years (only eight made it as far as the final exam). As a student, Makarova lived in daydreams, executing steps on the wrong foot, confusing arm positions, forgetting choreography as soon as she'd learned it. Nevertheless, she became the protégée of Natalia Dudinskaya, the Kirov's prima ballerina. For her graduation performance, Makarova danced Giselle, which is hardly a student's role, and scored her first great success. Here in the States, Makarova has come to depend on the careful coaching and watchful eye of Elena Tchernichova, a former fellow dancer at the Kirov, an émigré, now ballet mistress at A.B.T. Tchernichova, a product of the same Vaganova schooling, often gives Makarova private lessons, rehearses her in whatever ballet is at hand, puts her through a warm-up before the performance.

In 1976, Makarova married Edward Karkar, a San Francisco industrialist of Russian descent. In 1978, she gave birth to a son, Andrew ("Andrushka"), whose christening, with Rudolf Nureyev, former King Constantine of Greece, Marcia Kubitschek, Jacqueline Onassis, and Anne Getty for godparents, surely rivaled the Princess Aurora's.

With Baryshnikov in *Giselle*. Paris, 1977.

◄Dancing Jerome Robbins' *Other Dances* at Le Carré du Louvre with
Baryshnikov. Paris, 1977.

*Giselle.* Paris, 1977.

With Anthony Dowell after a performance of *Swan Lake*. Washington, 1980.

With Dowell after a performance of *Fantaisie Sérieuse*. New York, 1980.

Warming up, minutes before appearing on stage. This ritual of physical ▶
as well as psychological preparation is traditionally a private time.

◀preceding page:

Leopold Allen applying finishing touches to her wig before an appearance in Kenneth MacMillan's *Manon*. Washington, 1980.

Makarova rarely misses a class and always practices alone if she does.

Rehearsing *Swan Lake* with Godunov. Washington, 1980.

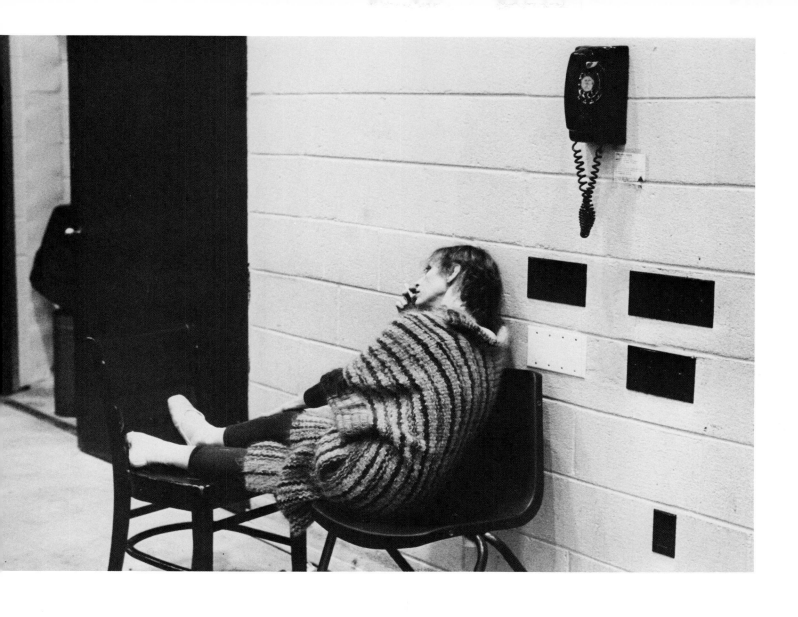

◄ Watching a rehearsal for *La Bayadère* with an especially
. critical eye  since Makarova herself was restaging it. The
American premiere was performed in New York in 1980.

Signing autographs.

Outside the Kennedy Center. Washington, 1980.

Three months pregnant with her son Andrew. (Makarova danced
practically every night of the American Ballet Theatre's European tour.)
Le Carré du Louvre, Paris, 1977.

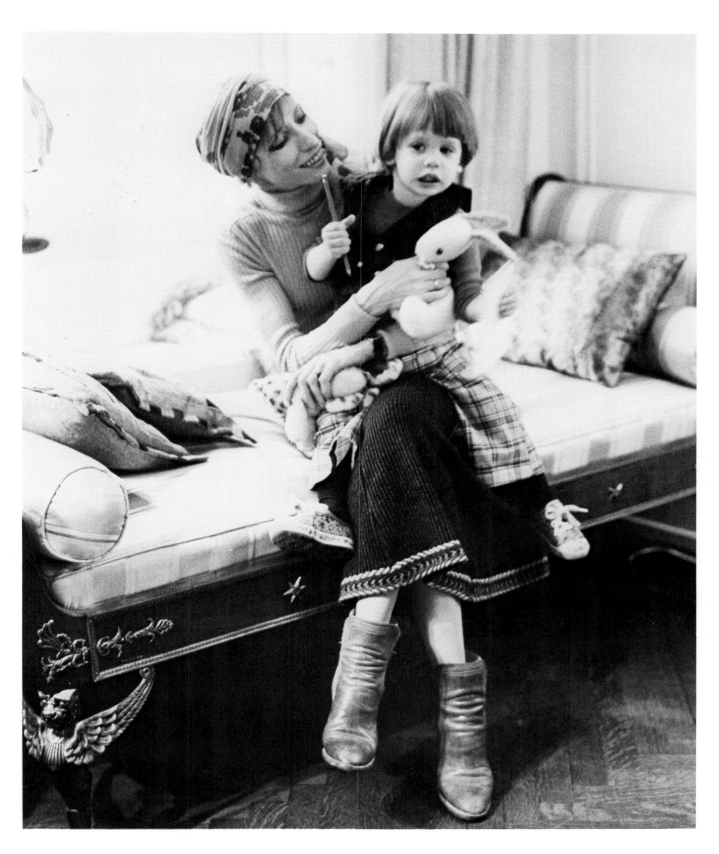

Makarova at home with Andrew in her apartment, which she shares with
her husband Edward Karkar. New York, 1980.

With set designer Oliver Smith and Lucia Chase, artistic director of the American Ballet Theatre, at a party given by Dance patroness Genia Doll following a performance of *Fantaisie Sérieuse*.

◄Costume fitting for Lorca Massine's *Fantaisie Sérieuse*. New York, 1980.

Born in 1959, Patrick Dupond is the youngest *étoile* of the Paris Opera Ballet. In 1976, he left Paris for the first time—for Varna, Bulgaria, where he represented France in the International Ballet Competition and won the gold medal in the junior division. For the fourth time in ten years, the Varna judges also awarded the special citation for technical excellence—again, to Dupond. (The three before him were Vladimir Vasiliev, Mikhail Baryshnikov, Fernando Bujones.) Dupond, then a member of the Paris Opera corps de ballet, was the first French dancer ever to win a gold medal at Varna. He was instantly proclaimed a star.

The Paris Opera, however, was not so easily won over; Dupond could wait his turn, like everybody else, advancing one rank at a time, taking the routine annual examinations required for promotion. When, later that same year, Dupond danced his exam on the stage of the Opéra Comique, the audience, which had been instructed to remain silent and impartial, burst into applause. Dupond was duly promoted to the rank of *coryphée.*

As a child, he was, by his own description, short and fat, with big flat feet. An overabundance of energy made for discipline problems—he was taken from one school to the next, made to try judo, soccer, any sport that might subdue him. Had he not eventually made his way to dance, he says, he would have become a pole vaulter.

At the age of ten, he took his first dance lesson and immediately ran home to tell his parents that dance would be his profession. He began studying with Max Bozzoni, a private teacher with whom he still works regularly, and, one year later, was admitted as a *petit rat* to the Paris Opera Ballet School. There, Dupond's ballet classes were combined with the same rigorous academic curriculum followed by all French schools. By

# Patrick Dupond

the time students from the Paris Opera enter the corps de ballet, at age sixteen—Dupond, bending the rules, entered a year early, at fifteen—most have already passed their *baccalauréat,* a nationwide test prerequisite to a diploma.

Since his first dance class, Dupond has grown tall and strong. With sandy hair, blue eyes, and a naturally melancholy expression, he has been described by one French writer as *"un véritable* 'outsider.'" He is well proportioned and flexible, with a big jump and—still—uninhibited energy.

Dupond had assumed that being a member of the Paris Opera Ballet would mean dancing all the time, but during his first year in the corps, he found himself with too much time on his hands and not enough dancing. So Bozzoni suggested that he go to Varna. They worked together for two months on several of the standard "showcase" variations from the classical repertory, some of which he still dances during guest appearances.

Dupond's first parts in the Paris Opera came in two ballets by Roland Petit, *Symphonie Fantastique* and *Nana.* One French critic writes that Dupond dances *"avec un brio incroyable."* His free-lancing, as he calls it, is curtailed by the Opéra's policies, and the company itself rarely tours, so Dupond's appearances in the United States are infrequent.

But now, promoted to *étoile,* he is still the whiz kid of the company—eager, impatient, outspoken, with ambitions that far exceed Paris and, for that matter, ballet. He wants an international career, with major companies all over the world, in all the "prince" roles in the classical repertory. He is taking voice lessons, as preparation for any possible opportunity on Broadway, in musical comedy. But this inclination toward a peculiarly American brand of show business is, for the time being, an avocation; Dupond calls it "my secret garden."

Dancing in the world premiere of Nikolais' *Shema,* at the Paris Opera, 1980.

Dancing Roland Petit's *Le Fantôme de l'Opéra* at the Paris Opera. 1980.

At his dressing table before appearing in *Shema*. Paris, 1980.

Makeup.

Dupond's permanent dressing room backstage at the Paris Opera.

Rehearsing John Neumeier's *Vaslaw,* a tribute to Nijinsky, to whom critics
often compare Dupond.

Backstage at the Paris Opera. 1980. ▶

◂New York.▸

New York.

Lunching across from Lincoln Center. New York.

At home, Paris.

◄ The morning run for croissants with his dog, Mouche. Paris.

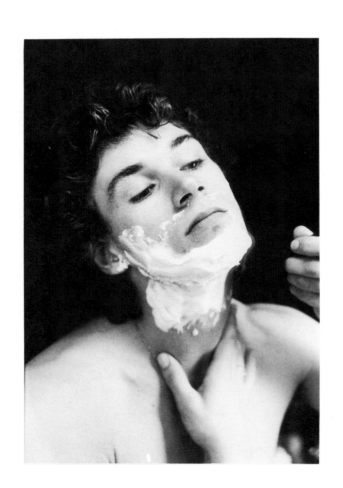

Patrick enjoying a moment of respite.

Patricia McBride is every child's idea of what a ballerina should be and, as her huge, loyal following at the New York City Ballet goes to show, she lives up to a good many grown-ups' expectations as well. As Swanilda in *Coppélia,* the ballerina in *The Steadfast Tin Soldier,* Columbine in *Harlequinade,* she becomes a doll, with delicately tapered arms and legs, an exaggerated instep on pointe, an arabesque that seems to come from the middle of her back, and a high forehead, wide eyes, a beaming smile. The first thing anyone sees the moment McBride steps out onstage is her face, which, with her beautiful, finely chiseled features, seems as clear to the audience in the fourth ring as to those in the front row.

As an opera singer fills a theater with his voice, McBride projects her dancing to the top of the highest balcony. Unlike Allegra Kent, Suzanne Farrell, Merrill Ashley—all fellow N.Y.C.B. ballerinas—she dances straight to the audience, but without delivering a sales pitch for the choreography, which, she seems confident, can speak for itself. So, in George Balanchine's *Baiser de la Fée,* as the Pearly Queen in the "Costermonger Pas de Deux" in his *Union Jack,* or dancing to George Gershwin's "Fascinatin' Rhythm" and "The Man I Love" in *Who Cares?,* McBride brings to the stage a warm radiance and a wit that are genuine, her own. But, for all her ingenuous charm, there is nothing simple about the person she is onstage: she seems somehow to have become a woman and all the while remained a girl.

As a girl, McBride studied ballet with a local teacher chosen by her mother and grandmother, who went comparison-shopping by attending recitals at several schools. When she was twelve years old, she was urged—by that same teacher, who had worked with her privately—to study in New York. So, twice a week, McBride's mother drove her from Teaneck, New Jersey, which was home, into the city for classes. One year later, she auditioned for the School of American Ballet and was offered a scholarship. McBride found the competition in the school exhilarating, the teachers inspiring: Pierre Vladimiroff would assign his students combinations from old ballets, Felia Doubrovska showed them the meaning

## Patricia McBride

of elegance. Melissa Hayden, then a principal dancer with the N.Y.C.B., was her idol.

McBride botched her company debut as an apprentice, in Balanchine's *Symphony in C*—off on the wrong foot, on the wrong beat—but was taken into the corps anyway. In 1959, when Balanchine called her out of the ranks and made a Chinese dance on her and Nicholas Magallanes for *Figure in the Carpet,* she was seventeen years old. Her progress came early, in small roles, then with a promotion to soloist and, a year later, to principal. In the years that followed, during the 1960s, the winning combination was McBride and Edward Villella, well matched in size and in style. The outlines of their partnership are preserved in the jazzy, exuberant roles Balanchine created for them in "Rubies."

Since Villella's retirement, McBride has danced with Helgi Tomasson, Mikhail Baryshnikov, Peter Martins, Jacques d'Amboise, among others, and Jean-Pierre Bonnefous, her husband, who first came to the N.Y.C.B. as a guest artist on leave from the Paris Opera and decided to stay. They married in 1973. Bonnefous, whose dancing has since 1979 been curtailed by an injury, has turned to choreography, and McBride sometimes dances the lead in his ballets, as she did in 1981, for his *Othello,* in St. Louis.

In 1974, when Alexandra Danilova and Balanchine collaborated on a new production of *Coppélia* for the New York City Ballet, it was McBride and Gelsey Kirkland who were chosen to dance the lead role of Swanilda. McBride felt privileged to become part of the tradition that ballerinas establish by passing along their roles (Danilova was the great Swanilda of her day). When, just before the premiere, Kirkland left the company to join A.B.T., *Coppélia* became McBride's ballet. Today, although she sometimes shares the role, no one disputes her claim to it. McBride is still very much in the forefront of the City Ballet, and for the company's Tchaikovsky Festival, in 1981, d'Amboise made her a new ballet, in *Scherzo Opus 42.* In addition, she makes guest appearances all over the world, getting to know and work with dancers—Godunov, for instance—who otherwise might never cross her path, performing in roles—like the Princess Aurora—she would never have the chance to dance at home.

◄Dancing *Tchaikovsky Piano Concerto No. 2* with her husband and fellow member of the New York City Ballet, Jean-Pierre Bonnefous. New York, 1976.

With Bonnefous performing *Opus 19/The Dreamer*. Paris, 1980.

With Bonnefous dancing a piece from *Who Cares?* for French television.
Paris, 1977.

With Helgi Tomasson after a performance of *Le Baiser de la Fée*.
Paris, 1977.

Makeup for *The Cage*.

Whereas male dancers may require as little as half an hour for makeup, the women often need at least two or three hours in which to apply all the different layers, each of which has to dry before the next can be put on.

In her dressing room backstage at the Champs Elysées Theatre.
Paris, 1980.

With Bonnefous checking their schedules. Times for classes and
rehearsals are rarely posted more than two days in advance.
New York State Theater, 1976.

Rehearsing *Le Baiser de la Fée* with Helgi Tomasson. Paris, 1980.

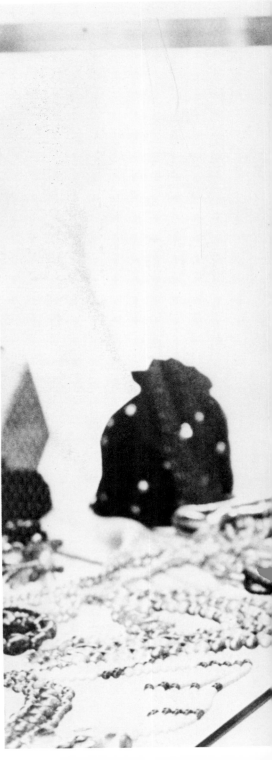

At the *Deux Magots* café in Paris.

McBride browsing at Yves Saint Laurent. Paris, 1980.

New York, 1976.

McBride and Bonnefous at home. 1980.

With Jean-Pierre and their cats.

◄With her Pekinese, LuLu.

At home with her husband.

With Jean-Pierre at Paris' Orly Airport.

For a week in August, 1979, Alexander Godunov instigated what spy novelists call "an international incident," a standoff between the United States and the U.S.S.R., during which the plane carrying his wife, a dancer with the Bolshoi Ballet, back to Moscow was detained for three days on a runway at Kennedy Airport. When finally it was ascertained to everyone's satisfaction that she was returning to Russia voluntarily, the plane took off and Godunov, by then famous as a defector, set about establishing himself as a dancer.

Like Natalia Makarova, Mikhail Baryshnikov, Rudolf Nureyev, and other Russian dancers who have defected to the West, Godunov is quick to insist that his decision to leave Russia was made on artistic, not political, grounds. As a principal dancer with the Bolshoi in Moscow, he danced leading roles in *Swan Lake,* the full-length *Don Quixote, Les Sylphides, Giselle,* the modern and Soviet works in the repertory. He partnered Maya Plisetskaya, who took him along on European tours and, in 1974, to America, and chose him for the filming of her ballet *Anna Karenina.* Godunov had an apartment of his own (which

is not usual, even for favored dancers, in Russia), a car, a sufficient salary, job security—even after a dancer's performing career is ended, his future (a pension, perhaps a teaching position) is seen to by the state. When Godunov decided to leave Russia, it was for the variety of dance forms, the freedom of choice, and even the risks the West had to offer.

Nevertheless, having sought and been granted asylum in the United States, Godunov suddenly found his dancing career in limbo. He joined the American Ballet Theatre during a layoff period, prolonged by a labor dispute. For four months, he did not perform; he rehearsed, but rarely, since A.B.T. management had locked the dancers out of their studios. At last, the disputes were settled and Godunov made his long-awaited debut, but not without dissent from some of the critics. After so long a period of restricted activity, he was not at the top of his form. So he was obliged to prove himself gradually, over the course of the next few months, the next year, in several performances. The road to the summit was uphill.

His height (over six feet tall), stubborn chin, and long

# $\mathcal{A}$ l e x a n d e r $\mathcal{G}$ o d u n o v

blond hair give Godunov the sort of good looks epitomized by Prince Valiant—youthful, heroic. But as roles in ballets by George Balanchine, Jose Limon, Glen Tetley make new, different demands on him, the emphatic, rock-star charisma that audiences thrilled to in his performances with the Bolshoi has been tempered by a more finished line and lyrical phrasing. Since his debut here, his technique has grown stronger and more precise. Guest appearances all over the world have kept him dancing more often than he did in Russia. The hardest adjustment he's faced has been to the quicker pace of life—and of dancing—in America.

Godunov was born in 1949, on an island near Japan, where his father was stationed with the Russian army. When he was a year old, his mother, who worked as a railroad engineer, took him and his older brother to her home in Riga, Latvia. There, at the Choreographic School, at age nine, Godunov began his ballet training. Like his fellow classmate Mikhail Baryshnikov, Godunov was short for his age; the two of them shared their worries. Told that tomato juice would make them grow tall, they drank it by the gallon. Told that sleeping on soft

beds would stunt their growth, they replaced their mattresses with boards. When, after one year at the Kirov School in Leningrad, Baryshnikov came home to Riga, he was taller than Godunov. It wasn't until almost two years later that the tomato juice and the boards began to take their prescribed effect and Godunov grew, almost overnight, to his present height.

After six years at school in Riga, Godunov dreamed of dancing with the Bolshoi, but first joined the ballet company formed by Igor Moiseyev, founder of the renowned Russian folk-dance troupe. During the three years Godunov danced with the Moiseyev Young Ballet, he tried—unsuccessfully—to make a move to the Bolshoi. They accepted him finally when, having left Moiseyev, he was being sought by the Soviet army as a draft evader (dancers are exempt from compulsory military service only as long as they keep dancing); the Bolshoi heard his plea and hired him in 1971. He made his debut in *Swan Lake,* as Siegfried, passing right over the ranks of the corps.

In 1973, Godunov entered the Second Moscow International Ballet Competition, in which he and another

Bolshoi dancer, Vyacheslav Gordeyev, shared the gold medal. In 1974, he came to the United States, touring with an ensemble titled Stars of the Bolshoi Ballet, headed by Plisetskaya. In Russia, Godunov partnered the Bolshoi's best ballerinas—Nina Sorokina, Marina Kondratieva, Ludmila Semenyaka, Plisetskaya. Since joining A.B.T., he's been paired with Natalia Makarova, Cynthia Gregory, Martine van Hamel, Magali Messac. And, of course, the company's direction is now in the hands of his old classmate Baryshnikov.

Dancing *Le Corsaire* at the 1980 Summer Festival in Carpentras, France.

Makeup just before appearing in his first American *Giselle*. Washington, 1980.

◄Backstage, just before the second act of *Giselle*. Washington, 1980.

Makeup for *Le Corsaire*.

Exuberant just after a sell-out performance of *Le Corsaire.* Washington, 1980.

Rehearsing *Swan Lake*. New York, 1980.

With Martine Van Hamel at a rehearsal for *Swan Lake*. New York, 1980.

Rehearsing *Giselle* with Makarova. Washington, 1980. ▶

Leaving the Opera House at Washington's Kennedy Center after his ▶
performance of *Giselle*. 1980.

Entering Genia Doll's apartment for a party following the world premiere of *Fantaisie Sérieuse*. New York, 1980.

Traveling.▶

At a post-performance party with Ghislaine Thesmar. 1980.

Godunov sampling American products.

Ghislaine Thesmar's father was a French diplomat, and his duties took his family to the most far-flung parts of the world—Peking, where Ghislaine (an only child) was born, in 1943, Havana, Indonesia, India, Morocco. In Havana, when Ghislaine was only five or six years old, her mother took her to see Alicia Alonso dance: her fascination with ballet was immediate, but short-lived. No sooner had she begun lessons with Alonso's sister in Cuba than the family packed up and moved to Indonesia. Ghislaine promptly forgot everything she'd learned. A few years later, living in India, she was enrolled in an English school, with a class schedule that included tap dancing and Scottish jigs. But clearly none of this was making Ghislaine into the French girl she was born to be, so, at the age of fourteen, she was sent by her parents back to Paris, to live with her grandmother and acquire some sense of what it means to be French and a better command of the language, which, she claims, she could hardly speak.

Paris was cold and lonely, and ballet lessons were the only consolation. But before too long, Ghislaine's father was transferred to Morocco, where she moved to re-join her parents and continue her dance lessons with a former ballerina from the Paris Opera. The teacher took an interest in her, and the two of them worked steadily together. So it was on her teacher's advice that Ghislaine entered the competition for entrance into the Paris Conservatory when, in 1958, her parents moved back to the capital. Of the two hundred girls who applied, five were chosen. The first was Ghislaine.

The Conservatory provided both an academic education and ballet training, all under government auspices. When Thesmar was graduated, at the age of eighteen, she decided against auditioning for the Paris Opera Ballet, which is for most Conservatory graduates the routine next step, and entered the corps of the Marquis de Cuevas' Grand Ballet instead. The company's repertory then included Bronislava Nijinska's *Sleeping Beauty*, ballets by Serge Lifar, George Balanchine, and others; among the guest artists were Yvette Chauviré and Rudolf Nureyev, who had just defected from Russia. The following year, after De Cuevas' death, the company dis-

# Ghislaine Thesmar

banded. Thesmar, temporarily homeless, joined a small group of dancers formed by George Skibine to perform at the festival in Aix-en-Provence; one of the eight dancers in that group was Pierre Lacotte, whom she married six years later.

But in the meantime, Thesmar danced with Lacotte in his own small company, the national Jeunesses Musicales de France, touring seven months a year—one-night stands, four ballets a night. Exhausted by the constant touring and in need of a little artistic independence, Thesmar left after five years and went to work with Les Grands Ballets Canadiens and, later, with Roland Petit. But, she insists, it was Lacotte who forced her to go beyond the limits she'd accepted for herself, who gave her the distinct identity she has today.

Thesmar is a strong, light, quick dancer with exquisite feet, delicate pointes, long flowing arms, high extensions, and a winsomeness and sophistication in keeping with her own nature. Like so much of what France exports to the rest of the world, she is beautifully made.

When, in the early 1970s, Lacotte undertook research for a book about Marie Taglioni, he discovered manuscripts, notated in detail, for the original choreography of *La Sylphide* (choreographed for Marie by Filippo Taglioni, her father), which had its premiere at the Paris Opera in 1832. These manuscripts, along with descriptions of the first production's costumes and sets and the score (by Schneitzhoeffer), proved evidence enough for Lacotte to reconstruct the original *Sylphide* for French television, with Thesmar as the Sylph and Michael Denard as James. On the basis of the TV version, the Opéra asked Lacotte to stage the same production there and—an unprecedented gesture—asked Thesmar to appear in her same role, a French dancer as a guest artist on her native ground. She signed a contract for three performances. When it expired, in 1973, she was offered another—this one, for a permanent position as a principal dancer, an *étoile*.

A year or so later, George Balanchine went to Paris to set a few of his works on the Opéra ballet and chose Thesmar to dance the leads in *Chaconne, Agon, La*

*Valse,* and *Tzigane.* In 1975, at his invitation, she came to the New York City Ballet as a guest artist and learned no less than twelve of Balanchine's ballets.

Because the Paris Opera Ballet is such a large, unwieldy organization, it rarely tours, and American audiences are still awaiting the chance to see Thesmar dance in the context of her own company. But, until that day comes, she makes the trip on her own, as she did in 1980, when, for the Boston Ballet's production of Lacotte's *Sylphide,* she came and danced the Sylph, with Nureyev as James, on Broadway.

Dancing *Le Corsaire* at the 1980 Summer Festival in Carpentras, France.

In *La Sylphide,* choreography by her husband, Pierre Lacotte. With
Michaël Denard. Paris, 1981.

Makeup.

In her permanent dressing room at the Paris Opera. The stars are allowed to decorate their *loges* in any way they choose.

Resting in her dressing room just before a performance.

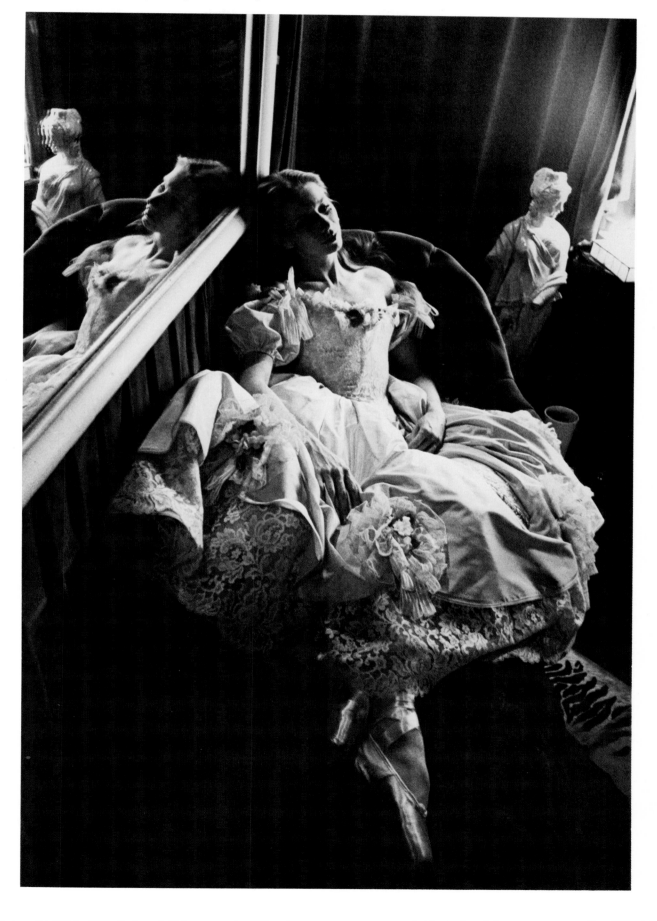

Going over the music with accompanist Babette Cooper.

Rehearsing *Marco Spada* with Nureyev at the Paris Opera. 1981.

With Godunov at the 1980 Summer Festival in Carpentras, France.

Class at the Paris Opera with Mademoiselle Yvette Chauviré. ▶

In front of her Paris apartment.

At Chanel's in Paris.

At home in Paris' historic Marais in the apartment which she shares with her husband and their cat.

With her pet rabbit, Brioche.

Their country retreat, a seventeenth-century château in central France.

Peter Martins is the matinee idol at the New York City Ballet. The role most often identified with him is Apollo—not because he happens to dance it especially well, which he does, but because he so completely looks the part. Tall and blond, with chiseled features, a jaw hewn out of rock, and a solid, broad-shouldered strength, he wins over audiences by self-effacement. In partnering, he calls attention to the ballerina; in a solo variation, to the steps.

Born in 1946, in Copenhagen, Martins was drafted into the Royal Danish Ballet School at the age of eight, when his mother took his two sisters to audition. The sisters didn't make it, but Peter, who'd been brought along instead of having been left with a baby-sitter, was invited to enroll because boys were scarce. The school provided both ballet and academic training, as well as the chance to perform—the children helped to fill out the crowd for large-scale ballets and operas at the Royal Theatre. Being a child and being a dancer were pretty much mutually exclusive, and Martins, given the choice at any time during his first five years in the school, would have preferred to be a child.

He changed his mind about dancing in classes taught by Stanley Williams (now on the faculty at the School of American Ballet). But his model was Erik Bruhn, a Danish *danseur noble* with an international career, who occasionally returned to Copenhagen for guest appearances. Martins studied him from a distance, tried to dance just like him. Finally, the probation on which Martins had lived for his first six years in the school was lifted; when he was eighteen, he was taken into the Royal Danish Ballet.

Williams left Denmark for the New York City Ballet. When he returned in 1967, as a guest teacher, Martins seized the opportunity: he asked Williams one night over dinner to find him a position dancing somewhere in the United States. The timing was uncanny. Before they'd finished eating, the phone rang: Vera Volkova, of the Royal Danish Ballet, calling for Martins to come to the theater right away for an audition. Jacques d'Amboise,

## Peter Martins

scheduled to dance the title role in Balanchine's *Apollo* for the Edinburgh Festival, was injured, and John Taras, the N.Y.C.B.'s ballet master, had come to Copenhagen in search of a replacement. Martins went to the theater, haughtily refused to audition on a full stomach, and got the job anyway, on Volkova's recommendation. The following day, he flew to Edinburgh, met George Balanchine and Suzanne Farrell for the first time, and rehearsed for one hour. The performance went fine. It was only afterward that Balanchine worked with Martins, dismantling his notion of the role, showing him where his version of the choreography was in error; Martins hungrily took it all in. Then, when d'Amboise's injuries continued, Martins was summoned to the City Ballet to partner Farrell. For two years, from 1967 to 1969, he shuttled back and forth between Copenhagen and New York. In 1970, he joined the New York City Ballet. The following year, Suzanne Farrell left.

By his own account, Martins spent his first three years in the company at The Ginger Man, a restaurant across the street from Lincoln Center. It wasn't until he finally realized what Balanchine was up to—experimenting, pushing the classical technique to its outermost limits—that his career at the City Ballet showed signs of falling into place. For the Stravinsky Festival, in 1972, Balanchine made two new works on him and Kay Mazzo—*Violin Concerto* and *Duo Concertante.* In *Tchaikovsky Concerto No. 2* (the old *Ballet Imperial,* revived in 1973 for Martins and McBride), with its overtones of *Swan Lake,* Martins became the ballet's center of gravity. As the repertory began to unfold for him and he acquired more roles, he danced them with absolute clarity and a characteristically pensive manner (head tilted, chin down, eyes down) that seemed serious, even reverent. In *Union Jack* and Jerome Robbins' *Fancy Free,* he could be very funny. Martins is perhaps limited in the roles he can play by his striking good looks; but his range, if not especially wide, is somehow deeper than most dancers'.

In 1975, Farrell returned to the New York City Ballet, making her re-entrance onstage on Martins' arm in Balanchine's *Symphony in C.* Balanchine then mounted his *Chaconne* and *Tzigane,* both made originally for other companies, on them, and they, with outstanding performances, laid claim to those two ballets as their own. Unlike many ambitious men eager to make their reputations as great dancers in their own right, reluctant to share the spotlight, Martins has always had an interest in partnering. As a child, he studied social dancing—the tango, waltz, foxtrot—which he likens to classical ballet pas de deux. The basic premise of both is, to his way of thinking, to provide a showcase for the woman. But when Martins dances with Farrell in *Chaconne, Tzigane, Agon,* "Diamonds," he does far more than display her line and extension. An intrepid ballerina who plunges into an *arabesque penchée* or a fish dive, blindly trusting her partner to catch her, Farrell has placed implicit faith in Martins and he, in the single-minded way he handles her, instinctively anticipates her next move. His utter dependability seems to have given Farrell even more rope, to have urged her on to new recklessness. She, in turn, treats him with a tenderness that makes their dancing together an even exchange.

Married in Denmark, Martins is now divorced. His former wife is a dancer with the Royal Danish Ballet; his son, Nilas, born in 1967, is now a student at the company's school. As his father did, Nilas performs in the big ballets at the Royal Theatre. When Martins returned to Copenhagen in 1976, dancing as a guest artist in *The Nutcracker,* his son was on the same stage.

In 1978, Martins began a second career, as a choreographer, with *Calcium Light Night,* an idiomatic ballet to the music of Charles Ives, for Heather Watts and Daniel Duell. Under Balanchine's tutelage, he has continued making ballets ever since, setting works on the New York City Ballet and on students at the School of American Ballet for their annual graduation performances.

In Jerome Robbins' *Fancy Free.* Paris, 1979.

Dancing Balanchine's *Apollo* with Suzanne Farrell (left) and Lourdes Lopez. Paris, 1980.

With Baryshnikov in Jerome Robbins' *Other Dances*—intended as a joke
since this ballet is meant to be danced by a man and a woman. Paris, 1979.

Performing *Apollo*. Monte Carlo, 1978.

Makeup. Paris, 1980.

Rehearsing Balanchine's *Agon* with fellow member of the New York City ▶
Ballet, Heather Watts.

▲Rehearsing Balanchine's *Theme and Variations*. Paris, 1980.

Class with the New York City Ballet. Paris, 1980.

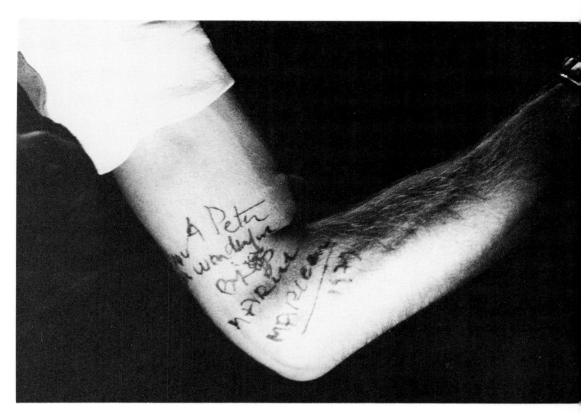

Marcel Marceau grabbed Martins' arm and autographed it in an
exuberant gesture of congratulations after watching Martins rehearse.

Backstage in his dressing room. Paris, 1979.

With Heather Watts. Paris, 1980.

Paying homage to Diaghilev in Monte Carlo. 1978.

Fitting at Valentino Più. Paris, 1980.

New York.

Cynthia Gregory is a dancer who, by virtue of her height and her dazzling technique, often seems formidable onstage. She can balance forever, turn on pointe so slowly that a *pirouette* becomes an unsupported *promenade.* When, as the Black Swan, she swings into double turns *à la seconde,* her leg slashing the air around her, the ferociousness contained in that one step is terrifying. Nature seems to have cast Gregory in certain roles—as Odile *(Swan Lake),* as Myrtha (the Queen of the Wilis, in *Giselle),* most recently, as the Siren in George Balanchine's *Prodigal Son.* Her shyness offstage sometimes becomes aloofness in performance. But, aware of the effects of her size and strength, Gregory has set about developing the less obvious aspects of her dancing—depth of character, expression in phrasing. And, in such unlikely roles as Odette *(Swan Lake),* Giselle, Raymonda, Swanilda *(Coppélia),* the Sylph *(La Sylphide),* she has succeeded. Still, to the minds of most of the dance audience, what makes Gregory remarkable is her calm, aristocratic manner, the capacity to channel her energy and passion for a role into the dancing itself.

Gregory was born in Los Angeles, in 1946, to Greek parents. In California she began dancing, taking class from Carmelita Maracci, who, she says, taught her musical phrasing, and taking notes every time the Royal Ballet and the New York City Ballet came to town. At eighteen, with a more or less fully formed technique, Gregory was already a soloist with the San Francisco Ballet and a principal dancer with the San Francisco Opera. When Margot Fonteyn and Rudolf Nureyev arrived for a guest engagement, Gregory dogged their every move, watching rehearsals, stationed in the wings. Fonteyn inspired Gregory to think about dancing in a wholly different way—how to shape certain steps and lines, how to make breathtaking effects. This much she could practice herself, alone in a studio. But that wasn't all: Gregory was overwhelmed by Fonteyn's partnership with Nureyev, by what happened between them when they danced together, and it created in her a (still unsatisfied) romantic longing for the perfect partner of her own. She is painfully aware that no great ballerina makes a career on solo variations, that the right partner can

# *C*ynthia *G*regory

bring out hidden aspects of a woman's dancing. Then, too, as an actress, Gregory depends on a leading man to inspire in her a greater sense of her own character, to provoke the sort of dramatic exchange actors rely on with one another as a matter of course.

Gregory has looked to different partners during her career to help her shape different roles: there is no one dancer who seems her perfect complement in every ballet. Since joining A.B.T. in 1965, she's danced a long list of roles that range from ingenue to femme fatale, from Caroline in Antony Tudor's *Jardin aux Lilas* to Medusa in his *Undertow,* with nearly as many partners—some of them brought in as guest artists, at Gregory's request. In flashy, showstopping turns like *Grand Pas Classique,* it was, during the 1970s, Ted Kivitt who would urge her on. That same edge has more recently been provided by Fernando Bujones, who is Gregory's match in technical feats. But, as she herself admits, competition simply isn't appropriate to every role.

However shy in personal matters, Gregory is outspoken when it comes to professional issues, like

A.B.T.'s treatment of American dancers; like Bujones, she has persistently campaigned for more roles and wider recognition for Americans in the company, at a time when the spotlight seemed trained on Russian defectors and guest stars imported from abroad. But, though Gregory's negotiations with Ballet Theatre management were often tense, their differences were always resolved.

In 1975, at the age of twenty-nine, Gregory quit dancing. Not for lack of money or performances, but for personal reasons, some of them mysterious even to her—she knew only that she'd begun to hate to dance. She returned to Los Angeles with her husband-to-be, John Hemminger, a musician. They married, bought a house, launched into a way of life that had nothing to do with ballet. Eventually, both missed the fast pace of life in New York and they began to make their way back to the city. Gregory, for whom life in New York had always meant dancing, resumed classes and her contract with A.B.T. So, after a year's sabbatical, she found herself once again in the studio, where she belonged more clearly than ever before.

▼Dancing *Tchaikovsky Pas de Deux* with Bujones at Le Carré du Louvre. Paris, 1977. ▶

Dancing a solo which Gregory choreographed herself for a gala at the
Met in New York.

Dancing the Rose Adagio for the American Ballet Theatre's fortieth anniversary gala. New York, 1979.

◄Makeup for *La Bayadère.*

Laughing with makeup artist Leopold Allen.

At the Russian Tea Room with her husband and manager, John
Hemminger, and the director of the Vienna State Opera.

Leaving the theater after a performance of *La Bayadère*.

Rehearsing Jose Limon's *The Moor's Pavane* with Erik Bruhn. Paris, 1977.

Class with Richard Thomas. This studio belonged to Balanchine when he
was first starting out.

On tour with the American Ballet Theatre in the summer of 1977,
shivering during a rehearsal break.

◄ After class.

New York.

At home.

◀Lunching with her husband at the health club on the top floor of their apartment building. New York.

Fernando Bujones, born in 1955, in Miami, of Cuban parents, moved with his mother to Cuba at the age of five. Because he was such a thin child, a doctor suggested exercise to encourage his appetite, and Fernando's exercise was ballet. After the Cuban revolution, he and his mother returned to Miami, joining his cousin, Zeida Mendez, a former dancer with Alicia Alonso's Ballet Nacional de Cuba, who coached Fernando in his dancing. When Jacques d'Amboise, a principal dancer with the New York City Ballet, came to town for a guest appearance, Mrs. Bujones, who was stage-managing the theater, asked that he audition her son. As a result, Fernando, then eleven years old, was offered a scholarship to the School of American Ballet's summer session and, at the summer's end, a full scholarship, renewed every year for the next five years.

Bujones cites three of his teachers at S.A.B.—and, of course, Mendez, who has stayed by his side as his coach—as the decisive influences on his dancing. From Stanley Williams, he learned clean execution and the Bournonville style, which is built on jumps and beats. From André Eglevsky, male strength and a noble stage presence. From Alexandra Danilova, grace. And from Mendez, whose demands are merciless, stamina.

Upon graduation, Bujones joined American Ballet Theatre, where, after a few months in the corps, he was handed soloist roles and, soon, principal roles. In 1974, with seven of the most difficult male variations in all ballet in his repertory and with Mendez in tow, he went off to the Varna Competition in Bulgaria and won a gold medal. But before he could return to the United States, Mikhail Baryshnikov defected to the West and, in some ways, stole Bujones' thunder. Bujones and Mendez, as it turned out, had timed their homecoming none too soon: they took a taxi straight from Kennedy Airport to Lincoln Center and arrived just in time to see Baryshnikov's debut with A.B.T.

There followed a series of brash interviews in which

# Fernando Bujones

Bujones compared his dancing to Baryshnikov's and, invariably, it was Bujones who came out on top. His braggadocio, in the press and onstage, alienated a large part of the ballet audience. The other part, however, was sufficiently impressed with his technical prowess to overlook the boasting.

Bujones' virtuosity, seemingly complete as early as his debut in the S.A.B. workshop, consists of well-turned-out strength, clean beats, an easy jump, sustained line, a high *relevé,* and multiple turns. With stamina enough for two dancers and a rare sense of musicality (he plays the piano), he shapes his dancing with clear positions in the air. A series of seven or nine *pirouettes* may end in a diminuendo, tapering off to a balance. Already he has danced every major role in the classical repertory— Siegfried *(Swan Lake),* Albrecht *(Giselle),* Colas *(La Fille Mal Gardée),* James *(La Sylphide),* Solor *(La Bayadère),* Don Basilio *(Don Quixote)*—as well as leads in ballets by George Balanchine, Antony Tudor, and Jerome Robbins.

Though Ballet Theatre is still home, he makes the international rounds in guest appearances with the Stuttgart, Berlin, Paris Opera, London Festival, and Brazilian ballets.

While performing in Rio de Janeiro, he met Marcia Kubitschek, daughter of the former president of Brazil. Married in 1980, they now live in New York with her two daughters by a previous marriage (one of them, a student at S.A.B.). Bujones has lately gone into business— speculating in real estate and marketing T-shirts and video cassettes that teach ballet technique.

Critics have begun to remark on a new maturity in Bujones' dancing; his audacity seems to have abated. But the bravura is intact. "Competitive" is a word he likes to describe his own approach to dancing, and, for all its athletic connotations, it goes a long way toward explaining the course of Bujones' career and the excitement that audiences so consistently find in his performances.

Dancing *La Sylphide* at Sadler's Wells. London, 1979.

After seeing Bujones in *La Sylphide,* London critics dubbed him "The Flying Bujones."

In *La Bayadère* with Marianna Tcherkassky at the Le Carré du Louvre. Paris, 1977.          Makeup for *La Sylphide*. ▶

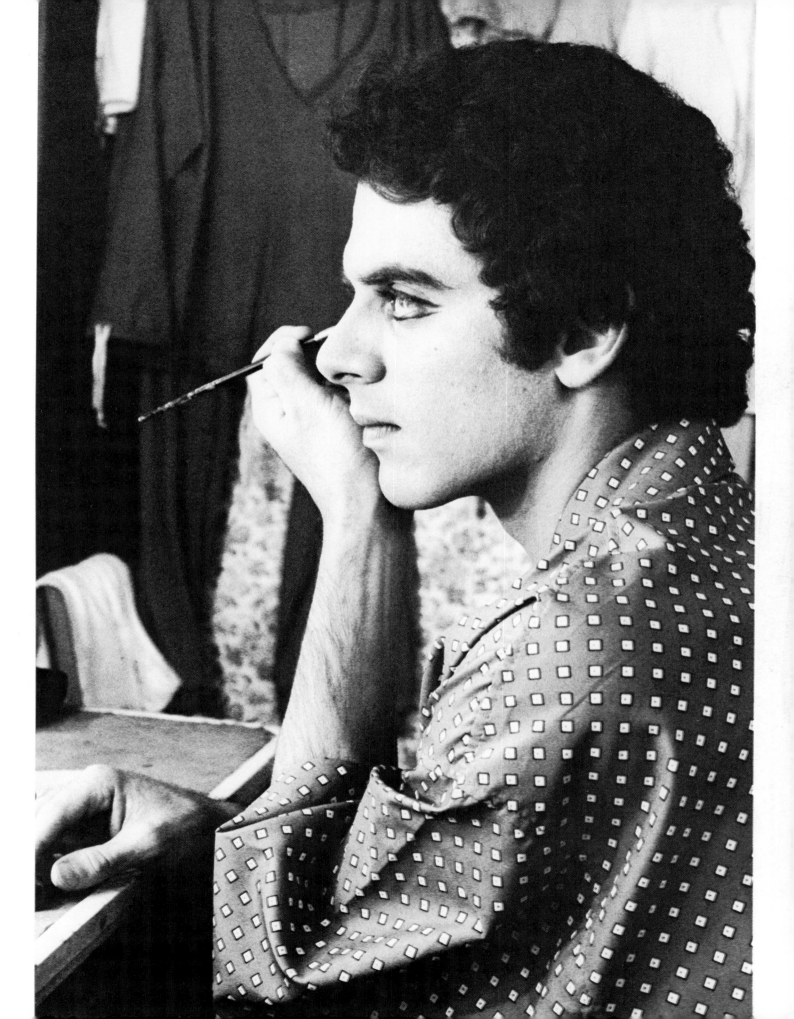

In his dressing room following a performance of *La Sylphide,* his costumes hanging on the wall.

Rehearsing *La Sylphide* with Sally Collard-Gentle.

Rehearsing with fellow members of the American Ballet Theatre, Kristine Elliott (left) and Marianna Tcherkassky.

Having his picture taken backstage with a fan. New York.

Class with the Scottish Ballet in London. 1979.

During a rehearsal break at Sadler's Wells. London, 1979.

With Dame Margot Fonteyn backstage after a performance of *La Sylphide*. London, 1979.

During a break at the Paris Opera. 1977.

Traveling in England.

With his fiancée, Marcia Kubitschek, the daughter of the ex-President of Brazil.  Versailles,1979.

Regent Street shopping. London, 1979.

Playing chess.

At home.

Like Ghislaine Thesmar, Martine van Hamel grew up all over the world: her father, like Thesmar's, was a diplomat. Born in Brussels, in 1945, she began ballet classes at the age of four, in Copenhagen; two years later, she studied Javanese dance in Indonesia; then ballet once again, in The Hague. From there she moved to Venezuela, where her family—two older brothers, a father who played the viola, a mother who played piano and violin—settled for three years. When the time for the next move—to Canada—came, Martine was thirteen. Her teacher in Caracas, Henry Danton, took some photographs of her dancing to New York, and on the basis of those alone, she was offered scholarships to the School of American Ballet and the American Ballet Theatre School. She declined both, in favor of staying with her family and studying ballet along with academics at the Toronto Academy, the training ground for the National Ballet of Canada.

In her senior year at the school, Van Hamel danced the Sugar Plum Fairy in the N.B.C.'s *Nutcracker.* After graduation she joined the company—as a soloist. Soon she was dancing leads in *Swan Lake, Giselle* (Myrtha), in ballets by Antony Tudor and George Balanchine. Then, in 1966, after a summer of studying in New York, Van Hamel was sent on a diplomatic mission of her own—to dance at the Varna Competition, in Bulgaria. In the under-twenty-one division, the men's prize went to a Russian dancer named Mikhail Baryshnikov. The women's prize went to Van Hamel, who was also awarded the overall prize for artistic interpretation. Taking her bow at the final performance, she slipped and fell.

As Van Hamel herself tells it, the glory turned her head, and both personally and professionally she needed to make a fresh start. She moved to New York, the city that beckons all dancers sooner or later, and auditioned for the American Ballet Theatre: the outcome was an offer to dance in the corps. But she had never danced in the corps before. She chose instead to join the Joffrey Ballet, where it soon became apparent that her style of dancing was completely at odds with that of the rest

## Martine van Hamel

of the company; she did three performances in the space of six months, then left. After yet another audition for Ballet Theatre, she took the corps contract she'd been offered in the first place, along with the promise of a few featured roles. But the promise wasn't always kept, and Van Hamel, for the next three years, seemed to fade in and out of focus. Her following was small but avid, comprised of A.B.T. regulars who make it their business to scan the corps for prospective ballerinas; her dancing at that time seemed—to everyone but Van Hamel, perhaps—one of those well-kept secrets bound to be made public before long.

To watch Van Hamel dancing now, it's hard to imagine how her amplitude, the absolutely grand scale of her movement, could ever have been embedded in the rows of the corps. With a tall, robust build, long-legged but firm, not willowy, with a strong supple back, she manages—as few dancers do—to deploy her whole body, every part of her moving at once. The beautiful lines most dancers show us only in poses Van Hamel miraculously sustains from one position to the next. A wonderful paradox underlies her dancing: her size, which might otherwise seem overwhelming, is contrary to her musicality, which is subtle, capable of the finest distinctions—little changes in rhythm or dynamics. If McBride is a small woman who dances big, Van Hamel is a large woman who knows how to make her dancing appear small.

In retrospect, Van Hamel's breakthrough came in the summer of 1974, when A.B.T. was in need of a Swan Queen and Van Hamel was cast in the role. She scored a huge success, especially in the "White Swan" pas de deux, where her natural gifts for adagio phrasing make the long violin melody sing. From then on, the roles came thick and fast—Myrtha, Raymonda, leads in Balanchine's *Theme and Variations* (in which her dancing is buoyed by Tchaikovsky's music), Tudor's *Jardin aux Lilas,* Harald Lander's *Études.* The list grows longer with every new season, and Van Hamel's fans are now legion. In 1979, she gathered together a group of dancer friends and formed an ensemble for performing solos and small ballets, some of them of her own choreography.

Performing *La Bayadère* with Patrick Bissell. Minneapolis, 1980.

◄ With Patrick Bissell dancing a pas de deux.

With Clark Tippet in Stravinsky's *Sacre du Printemps*. Paris, 1977.

After a performance of *Jardin aux Lilas*. Minneapolis, 1980.

With Leopold Allen before a performance of *Jardin aux Lilas*.
Minneapolis, 1980.

◄Washington, 1980.

Rehearsing a pas de deux. Minneapolis, 1980.

First professional meeting with Godunov and first rehearsal for *Swan Lake*. New York, 1980.

Class with the American Ballet Theatre. Minneapolis, 1980.

Minneapolis, 1980.

Breakfast on the road with
fellow dancer Kristine Elliott.

Being interviewed in her Minneapolis hotel room. 1980.

Returning home exhausted after a strenuous tour.

At home. New York, 1980.